Hot and Wet

by Carmel Reilly

OXFORD
UNIVERSITY PRESS
AUSTRALIA & NEW ZEALAND

It is hot.

The cat is on the deck.

It is wet.

The cat will nap in a box.

hot

The dog will sip at the tap.

wet

The dog is in a jacket.

hot

The fox is hot in the sun.

wet

The fox will run back to the den.

The vixen is in the den.

The vixen and cubs nap in the den.

cubs

hot

wet